How To Make Whiskey

A 7-step guide to making your own unique bourbons, ryes, and malts

HOW TO MAKE WHISKEY

A Step-by-Step Guide to Distilling Whiskey

By Bryan Alexander Davis

Head Distiller for Lost Spirits Distillery

This book is dedicated to Joanne Haruta, my amazing partner in business and in life. Joanne's tireless efforts have made this book and our distillery possible.

Special thanks to Jacqueline Davis, my mom, who edited this book.

"Always carry a flagon of whisky in case of snakebite, and furthermore, always carry a small snake."
– W. C. Fields

"If I cannot drink bourbon and smoke cigars in Heaven, then I shall not go."
– Mark Twain

"I should never have switched from Scotch to Martinis."
- Humphrey Bogart's last words

TABLE OF CONTENTS:

ABOUT THE AUTHOR

Bryan Davis Building The Massive Stills At Lost Spirits Distillery

Bryan Davis has been master distiller of two controversial and celebrated distilleries. He began distilling spirits in high school when obtaining a fake identification proved more difficult than one might expect. After a short stint as an art teacher, he returned to his first love—booze, and he has been hard at work making award-winning spirits ever since.

In his current role as Master Distiller for Lost Spirits Distillery: a boutique single malt whiskey house located in Monterey County, California, Davis has developed all of the recipes, and built (almost) all of the equipment from scratch. From hand-pounding the copper on the two-story stills at Lost Spirits, to re-coopering and charring his own casks, Davis has worked on each and every step of the whiskey-making process.

His work has been featured in *Wine Enthusiast Magazine*, the *NY Times*, *Forbes*, *Mutineer Magazine*, and countless other publications.

Besides distilling, Davis has spoken at multiple conferences about making spirits, and spent some spare time as a guest writer for *Mutineer Magazine*, covering topics related to the history of distilled spirits.

"I love what I do, and feel fortunate to have the opportunity to drink my life's work."

–Bryan Davis

FOREWORD

In buying this book, you have begun the first step on a long journey into a magical world where ordinary things like yeast, rye, and barley transform into extraordinary things like *Ardbeg Supernova*, and *Rittenhouse Rye*. If you are anything like I am, this obsession will consume most of your free time -- a tiny price to pay for the opportunity to command the incredible sorcery that is whiskey-making.

My obsession with distillation began as a teenager. Unable to get a suitable fake identification card, I made up for what I lacked in years with a homemade still, and plenty of closet space to set up a clandestine distillery. Since then, I have yet to find a reliable book on the topic. Unfortunately, the path to making your own whiskey remains clouded by a lot of misinformation, and a few potentially dangerous pitfalls. With this book, I am confident that not only will you make whiskey in a matter of days, but you will also be equipped with the knowledge to begin fine-tuning your whiskey into something extraordinary.

This book is designed to delicately balance the basics of whiskey making in each simple-to-read, plain English section. However, in the advanced portions of each section I will go into the myriad of variables involved, and how to fine-tune them to get the results you want.

–Bryan Davis

PART 1: SAFETY

SAFETY

DO NOT SKIP THIS CHAPTER! I know you want to do it, but DON'T!

Distilling spirits is not as dangerous as you might think. With the help of this book and a little common sense, it can be done completely safely. However, there are a few precautions to keep in mind. In this section, we will cover the obvious, but often-understated flammability of alcohol, the toxicity of methanol (and how to not accidentally drink it) and the rare, but dangerous, pressure explosions. As long as you respect a few simple rules, you are nearly guaranteed to not poison your friends, or blow yourself up!

EXPLOSIONS & FLAMMABILITY

The primary danger in making your own whiskey is flammability and explosions. Both of these events are potentially fatal, and generally unpleasant. Near-death experiences can easily be avoided by applying some simple common sense.

It is important to understand that you are making a substance that is as flammable as gasoline. When the still first begins to run it can produce distillate as concentrated as 90% alcohol. When you buy a bottle of whiskey at the store, the strongest concentration you will likely encounter is 62.5 percent alcohol. Though still flammable at 62 percent, it is far more flammable at 90 percent alcohol. There is a reason you can run a car on this stuff!

When you are making your own spirits, the first part of the distillation will come off the still near 90 percent alcohol. Not only is this as flammable as gasoline, it is also in a vapor state as it passes through the still. This means that if you hold a match to the end of your still during the first distillation phase, it will EXPLODE, sending flaming alcohol everywhere, along with copper shrapnel made out of what used to be your beautiful (and expensive) still.

To avoid this most unfortunate and disfiguring outcome, you must take precaution against a few Darwinian mistakes. First, don't heat your still with a naked flame. Commercial open-flame heated stills have their condensers located 4 to 20 feet away from the flames. This prevents the liquid from being anywhere near the flames. Small home distillation units are not this big, and thus, your condenser will be too close to the flames to safely operate. An electric hot plate is a far safer option.

The second key to not blowing yourself up relates to the condenser. Since the alcohol vapor travels through the still at boiling temperatures, it needs to be cooled down into a liquid in the condenser. If you let the cooling water in your condenser overheat, the vapor will eventually pass through the cooling coil and out into the air as alcohol steam. This steam is obviously flammable/ explosive. The simple solution to this problem is to check your condenser temperature often, and **never** leave a still unattended. If the condenser overheats, and alcohol steam comes out of the condenser, calmly stop screaming, put out your cigar, turn off the still, and extinguish any sources of ignition nearby! Once you have extinguished any sources of ignition, add fresh cold water to the condenser.

NOTE: JOKES ASIDE, DO NOT SMOKE WHILE DISTILLING. SMOKING WHILE DISTILLING IS A DARWIN AWARD WAITING TO HAPPEN!

PRESSURE EXPLOSIONS

Though very rare, pressure explosions can, theoretically, happen if a still foams and clogs the neck or condenser plumbing. Usually, the cause is overfilling your still. The way to prevent the clogging problem is to only fill the still to a maximum of two-thirds full before starting it. However, even if it does clog, this is usually not a problem, since stills have been engineered to avoid exploding since the 1500s.

Well-made stills are usually sealed at the neck with flour paste. In the event of a plug, the still head simply pops off, releasing the pressure. Commercial stills have special pressure release valves. In either case, it is "generally" impossible for the still to build excessive back-pressure and explode.

However, if you built your own still (something that I don't recommend unless you have done a lot of research) and you have the head sealed on with bolts or something tougher than flour paste, it could plug and explode.

Once, I heard a story about a man in Norway who built his own 100-gallon still, sealing the head on with brass flanges and bolts. While it was running, he went to the store--a highly stupid thing to do--and returned to find he had actually shot the head of the still through his roof and into the back yard. A costly mistake, to be sure!

NOTE: I am unclear if homeowner's insurance covers exploding stills in the garage. I suggest that you consult your homeowner's policy, or your landlord, for further clarification.

HOW NOT TO GO BLIND

All those stories about people going blind during Prohibition are a bit misleading. Methanol is a definite poison, and it does cause blindness. However, you are far less likely to drink it than you might think. In fact, it's almost impossible for you to poison yourself making whiskey in small batches at home.

Though it is true that methanol is produced in trace amounts by yeast during fermentation, there is usually not enough produced in small batches (i.e. using a still that produces just a few gallons) to make anyone sick. Beer and wine are fermented the same way as distilled spirits, yet you never hear of anyone going blind after drinking a bottle of wine.

So you might ask: Where did all those tragic stories of people going blind during Prohibition originate? During Prohibition, "denatured" alcohol was sold as a degreaser. It was denatured by adding 10 percent methanol to it. This was to prevent mechanics from drinking the industrial alcohol they legally bought to degrease engines. At the time, it was a common practice for bootleggers to the attempt to remove the poison through distillation and sell the degreaser as "bathtub gin." When a bootlegger made a tragic mistake, the consequence was that people died or became permanently blind.

Notwithstanding, there are a few things to know about methanol, and how to safely avoid drinking it. Methanol (the poison) has a lower boiling point that ethanol (the drinking alcohol). Therefore, it comes off the still **first.** When you are distilling, you **always collect the first tablespoon of distillate per gallon of mash and throw it away.** This is called the "heads cut." The removal of the "heads" prevents you from drinking any methanol. Trace amounts of methanol in your spirit are the cause of those pounding headaches that occur during a hangover. Following this simple practice will protect you from both blindness and hangovers.

It is important to cover two scenarios that could result in a dangerous amount of methanol.

1. **Large Batches:**
   If you distill a large batch of spirits, such as 10 gallons of whiskey mash, then you would produce 10 tablespoons of "heads." If a person collected the "heads" and drank them, they could poison themselves. Think of it this way: if you drink a full bottle of wine you would ingest a small amount of trace methanol, perhaps enough to give you a pounding headache. However, it would not be enough to put you in a hospital. If you used a still to concentrate the trace methanol produced in 10 gallons of wine, you would have a dangerous quantity of the substance. Drinking that could actually kill someone. As a rule, DO NOT drink the "heads" from a distillation. They are absolutely poisonous. It is also important to dispose of them immediately so that no one accidentally drinks the "heads." "Heads" taste and smell just like regular alcohol, so you cannot tell the difference between methanol and ethanol by taste. Practically speaking, you can only tell which one you are distilling by when it exits the still.

2. **Spoilage Bacteria:**
   Certain bacteria can produce methanol. If your mash smells rotten and/or clearly has some strange rotting bacteria growing in it, do not distill and drink the product. While fermenting, your mash should smell like sweet, fruity beer. There will be more on identifying types of bacteria that will be covered later in this book.

PART 2:
TOOLS OF THE TRADE

Still Selection:

In order to make your own spirits, you must first possess a still. Choosing what type to buy is actually a bigger decision than you might think. Besides the range of costs, different stills will result in different flavor profiles. A typical hobby still will cost you about $450.00, so you want to think carefully about which design to buy, based upon what kind of flavor density you want. On one end of the spectrum is the traditional European alembic pot still (also sometimes called a cognac still), which makes a very dense, richly flavored spirit. This type of still is also quite beautiful, and can add a touch of elegance to any suburban garage. On the other end of the spectrum is a packed column, called the "modern moonshine still." This type will strip nearly all the flavor out of your whiskey, making something closer to gasoline than *Glenfiddich*. Between these two options are literally dozens of designs, each with its own set of pros and cons. To help you make an informed purchase, in this chapter we will cover the basic differences between each commonly available option.

Still Size:

When it comes to stills, size **does** matter, and in this case, bigger is **not** better. It takes some time to fine tune a recipe. Over the course of that time, you will run dozens and dozens of test batches. If you use a fifteen-gallon still, you will find yourself throwing away gallons and gallons of test batches, or giving them to friends until they develop liver damage. Raw materials are expensive. It's much better to work smaller when you are learning.

Waste is also an issue. Whenever I throw away a small test batch, I remember that there are thirsty bums in this world. I would not want it on my conscience that I am throwing away 2 gallons of whiskey, while they go sober!

All humor aside, a 2 to 3-gallon pot still is an ideal size for a hobbyist. A three-gallon still will produce approximately one bottle of 50 percent to 55 percent whiskey, per batch.

NECK HEIGHT:

The neck height of the still is a big issue. Rectification is the process by which alcohol and water are separated in the still. This happens when the heavier water vapor has to travel up a long neck. Over time, the heavier water vapor will actually cool and fall back into the pot, while the alcohol vapor can pass through the tall neck.

Taller-necked stills will produce stronger alcohol concentrations, but they will make less densely-flavored spirits. The positive side to tall necks is that they will remove many of the off-flavors produced by a less-than-successful fermentation. The negative side to tall necks is that they will remove the heavier, nutty or smoky flavors that you might want from your mash.

Your choice of still design will ultimately influence the character of your spirit. With a tall-necked still, you will have less undrinkable batches, but also less great ones. Personally, I am a proponent of short-necked European-style stills over their American rivals.

THE ALEMBIC POT STILL

Originally created by the Moors for the distillation of perfumes, the alembic may well be the oldest surviving still design. The one shown above is from my former distillery in Spain. The graceful lines of these "beauties" also make them the first choice of people decorating their homes with their stills. This type of still is readily available for purchase in Europe. Galicia, Spain, and Portugal commercially produce thousands of alembics every year. These types of stills can be bought online. *Hoga Company* and *Iberian Coppers* are two reliable, reasonably - priced suppliers.

The short necks of these stills ensure that a great amount of water (which contains additional flavors) passes through the still during the distillation. In the right hands, this type of still can produce some of the world's most richly-flavored, deep, and brooding spirits. However, despite the benefits of this design, there are some pitfalls. Mainly, these stills are very unforgiving. If there are any flaws in the fermentation process or the raw materials, these flaws WILL show up in your finished product.

If you are trying to ferment moldy bread and half rotten strawberries, this is not the still for you.

EUROPEAN WHISKY STILLS

Closely related to the alembic, these stills are the "weapon of choice" for Scotch whisky distillers. They work essentially like an alembic, except that the neck is about twice as tall, and the mouth is narrower. This causes some of the water in the vapor to condense and fall back into the pot.

The advantage of this still is that it is slightly more forgiving than an alembic, and makes the distillate a little crisper, helping the distiller to better distinguish what is happening during the distillation. Many years ago, during the American whiskey heyday, these stills were quite common in the United States. Today, they are no longer used here. I find this design to be a great choice for anyone seriously pursuing whiskey making (either American or Scotch). My own personal whiskey stills are a hybrid of this design.

If you plan to make brandy in addition to whiskey, I would stay with the alembic still, since it is more suitable for both. If you are only making whiskey, go for the European whiskey still. These are readily available for reasonable prices at *www.copper-alembic.com*

CLASSIC AMERICAN MOONSHINE STILLS

These are quite rare today. I actually own one that is a relic of Prohibition. They function in much the same way as an alembic still, except their extremely short neck causes them to be even less forgiving than an alembic. To make a classic moonshine still produce a palatable product, it usually requires a secondary chamber called a "thumper" or "doubler." This chamber earned its nickname because it thumps to a rhythm while distilling.

This secondary chamber is located between the still neck and the condenser. It is filled with either water or "low wines," and is heated by the vapor of the distillate. The distillate steam exits the main still and enters the doubler by bubbling through the water or low wines that are in the doubler. The doubler acts like a filter that cleans the distillate of many of the undesirable aromas from the mash. Traditional moonshiners link up a series of these doublers, sometimes as many as 6 of them, to produce true classic moonshine.

Having experimented with this design quite extensively, I can say that a classic moonshine still with two doublers can produce beautiful bourbons. However, to my knowledge, there are no companies commercially manufacturing and selling these for hobby distillers. *Iberian Coppers* does sell the design, but you would have to solder together your own doublers. It's not impossible by any means, but it would require some metal working skills. Just remember to use only silver-bearing, lead-free solder.

You can sometimes find relics of Prohibition for sale. However, you must be very careful, as many of the moonshiners used lead solder to join the copper together.

If you are a collector of classic Americana, and are brave enough to go down this road, I recommend purchasing a lead test kit. Hardware stores often carry a small rub-on kit designed for testing lead paint. Again, exercise extreme caution! Lead is very soluble in acidic solutions, and will build up in your body over time. A lead-soldered still can actually kill you. That being said, it can do wonders for your personality!

If you are a skilled metal worker, and wish to make your own still, roofing supply companies sell 4 x 10- foot copper sheets for about $250.00. If you are up to the task, you could solder a small still and two doublers together at bargain basement prices.

Just remember to use only silver bearing lead-free solder.

Photo courtesy of: *Fog's End Distillery*

These stills function much like a European whiskey still. They are characterized by their aesthetics. Typically, these are made from sheet copper welded together in sharp angular lines. They come fitted with a uniquely American "pipe in a pipe" condenser that requires an external pump and a water tank from which to circulate cooling water. For all intents and purposes, these are fine stills. It's mostly a choice of personal style. That is especially true if you're going to set it next to your 1932 coupe in the garage!

HOT PLATE

Once you have chosen your still, you will need to heat it. A simple hot plate, at a very low setting, is an effective and inexpensive way to mimic an open-flame distillation. The only drawback to this method (and open flames for that matter) is that if you are distilling a thick whiskey mash, it is very easy to burn the mash. You will know if you have burned the mash because you will notice black smoke coming out of your condenser, and a foul burnt taste in your whiskey.

If you plan to distill only strained, wort-based whiskeys, this is not so much of an issue. Even if you are distilling thick mashes, you can still make a hot plate work. You will, however, have to distill very slowly to avoid burning the mash.

Advanced:

How you go about heating your still can have as big of an effect on the flavor of the product as the still design. As an alternative to the hot plate, you could rig-up a tiny steam boiler from a pressure cooker. In this way, you could heat your still the way most commercial distilleries do.

To make a steam coil, drill two ¼" holes in the shoulders of the still. Buy a ¼" flexible copper tube from the hardware store. Wind the tubing into a coil and thread through the holes. Solder them tight with silver solder.

To connect the boiler to the coil, you will need to drill a hole in the stainless lid of the pressure cooker. Then braze ¼" brass fittings from the hardware store onto the pressure cooker lid, using 56% silver brazing rods. Once the fittings are installed, simply connect the coil to the pressure cooker and boil water in the pressure cooker. Though not an easy task, it is possible for skilled metal workers.

COOKING POT

You will need a large cooking pot to prepare your mash. It should be approximately the same size as your still. Some home-brewers may also have wort strainers to remove the grains at the end. If you do have a wort strainer, that's wonderful. If not, you can also use cheesecloth to accomplish the same thing.

FERMENTATION BUCKET

Homebrew shops sell all sorts of fancy mini-fermenters. What you really need is a bucket with a lid. Food grade plastic buckets work well, and all homebrew shops will have them. You don't need anything fancy, just a simple bucket.

SUGAR HYDROMETER (Saccharometer)

This is an invaluable tool that will tell you the amount of sugar (or potential alcohol) in your mash. This device will help you monitor the fermentation as it progresses. Any homebrew shop will have these for sale for a few dollars, since they are essential to making any alcoholic beverage.

ALCOHOL HYDROMETER

This is a valuable tool that will tell you the amount of alcohol in your distilled spirit. You cannot effectively make distilled spirits without one. Most homebrew shops will have these for sale for prices between $10.00 and $30.00.

GRADUATED CYLINDER

This is a polypropylene or glass measuring tube that you will use with your hydrometers to check the alcohol or sugar concentrations. Homebrew shops will always sell these.

ELECTRIC SPACE HEATER WITH THERMOSTATIC CONTROLS (OPTIONAL)

As you get more advanced, you may want to experiment with altered fermentation temperatures. The best way to do this is to place your fermentation bucket in a small closet with an electric heater, set to maintain at a certain temperature.

THERMOMETER

A thermometer with a temperature range from 75 degrees to 160 degrees Fahrenheit is essential.

YEAST

There are, literally, hundreds of commercially available yeast strains to choose. All of them will make a drinkable whiskey. Even *Laphroaig*, one of the world's greatest distilleries, publicly advertises that they use baker's yeast.

Each unique yeast strain will produce its own signature set of volatile acids and esters. Since these compounds play a major role in the flavor of your spirit, you could say that your choice of yeast strain is as important as your choice of still or mash.

There are two primary types of yeast strains. Lager yeast (also known as bottom-fermenting yeast) and ale yeast (also known as top-fermenting yeast.) For many years, these were thought to be different sub-species. However, they have recently been identified as both originating from the same sub-species (Saccharomyces Cerevisiae), so reading the Latin name on the packets won't do much good. In my opinion, it is best to avoid lager yeasts, as they tend to produce less volatile esters and acids—or, in short, a less complex whiskey.

Esters are the flavors of fruits and flowers in nature. They are formed when a volatile acid is bound to an alcohol molecule and an oxygen molecule. All yeast strains will produce some of them. However, some strains will make many more than others. Volatile acids are not palatable. However, in the aging process, they gradually bond with alcohol to form esters. Producing lots of volatile acids in your fermentation means that your whiskey will age more gracefully.

Ale yeasts produce a huge variation in volatile acid and ester profiles, from one strain to the next. You could, literally, experiment for a lifetime making different whiskeys just by changing yeast strains. One friend of mine has dedicated her life to collecting various yeast strains, and literally, has thousands of them in her laboratory. To make things more complicated, you can even cross breed different strains and make your own hybrid yeast strain!

Different strains WILL make different products. I am not going to tell you which one to choose. The world will be a richer place if you experiment for yourself. Simply ask your local homebrew shop for a list of their ale yeast strains, and begin experimenting. Tell them you want an "estery" profile.

I want to dissuade you from the popular missteps of *Turbo Yeast* or *Champagne Yeast*. These yeasts will give you a higher starting alcohol concentration, but at the expense of almost everything good that can come from yeast. In short, *Turbo and Champagne Yeasts* are great options for making fuel, but not a good choice for making whiskey.

FREEZE DRIED BACTERIA

All mashes will begin to grow bacteria as the yeast start to die (usually by the end of the second day of fermentation). Most of the time, the bacteria will be a strain of Lactobacillus -- the friendly bacteria we use to make cheese and yogurt. However, there are several evil bacteria strains, like clostridium, which can also show up at the end of fermentation. If you don't add your own bacteria to the mash, Mother Nature will select one for you, and there is a good chance that you won't like the one she chooses. If you want to experiment with adding your own bacteria, you can do so by buying packets of dried bacteria. I recommend browsing www.cheesemaking.com for ideas.

NOTE: Lactobacillus will also help prevent spoilage bacteria from taking over your mash.

Homebrew shops will often carry a few strains of bacteria for home wine makers and sour mash beer makers. Organic grocery stores will often carry cheese and yogurt making kits, each with their own unique bacterial combination. As long as you stay with the Lactobacillus family, you can't go too far wrong.

Bacteria strain choices can have a major impact on your whiskey, especially if you ferment for more than three days. Lactobacillus strains will produce lots of lactic acid, and lactic acid esters (notably tasting creamy and buttery). They also produce a cocktail of their own volatile acids, creating complexity in your whiskey (more on this later in the book).

POWDERED AMYLASE ENZYME

Amylase enzyme is the enzyme produced naturally in malted barley. It converts the starches in grains into fermentable sugars, and it is crucial to the fermentation process. Since the malted barley does not always contain a large amount of the enzyme, it is often beneficial to add extra. You can buy it in small bottles of powder at your local homebrew shop. Usually, ½ teaspoon added to a gallon is sufficient to increase your yield by 10 percent to 20 percent.

PART 3:
MAKING WHISKEY

STEP 1.
RECIPE SELECTION

Whiskey is a "catch all" term for a flavorful distilled spirit made from grain. Under that heading are dozens of different types and styles, each with its own signature flavor. Before you start making whiskey, you will need to decide on a type to make. In this chapter, I have outlined a series of basic recipes. Also, I have included some tips for experimenting with your own creations. Just remember that none of this is set in stone. Feel free to mix and match styles to create a new whiskey that is all your own. If you are lucky, you might create something that stands the test of time.

If you get lost in reading the recipes, don't feel bad. I wrote them for you to revisit after reading the next several chapters. They may include new vocabulary and things that don't yet make sense. Don't worry. It will all make sense later.

BOURBON WHISKEY:

Native to the United States, bourbon whiskey was invented as a substitute for cognac in the 19th century. At its best, bourbons are characterized by a rich caramel flavor, complicated by charred oak notes and dried cherries. There are two dominant sub-styles: high rye bourbon and wheated bourbon. *Four Roses* single barrel is a good example of the high rye style, whereas the *Pappy Van Winkle* line is a good example of the wheated variety. If those are too hard to get, you could use *Basel Hayden* (high rye) and *Woodford Reserve* (wheated) as substitutes.

27

By law, bourbon is 51 percent corn (maize), and must be aged in a new charred American oak cask. Typically, the recipes are closer to 65 percent to 70 percent corn, and always include some malted barley (since malted barley contains enzymes that convert starch to sugar). In addition, the recipes always include either rye or wheat, or both, as flavoring grains.

Basic Bourbon Recipe:

Ingredients:

1 gallon water

2 lbs. ground **untreated** cornmeal or polenta

½ lb. cracked malted barley

¼ lb. cracked rye berries

¼ lb. wheat flakes

Lalvin ICV-D21 yeast

Instructions:

1. Bring 1 gallon of water to 160 degrees. Stir in corn, followed by rye, wheat flakes, and finally barley. Hold at 152 - 155 degrees for 1 to 2 hours.

2. Cool the mash to 92 degrees. Transfer the resulting liquid and solids to your fermentation bucket. Add yeast. Ferment hot (85 degrees - 90 degrees) for 2 to 4 days.

3. Distill with all the grain and yeast from the bottom of the fermentation bucket added to the still. Distill your low wines to a total ABV (alcohol by volume) of around 30 percent.

4. Redistill the low wines and collect and discard 1 tablespoon of heads per gallon mash. Distill your finished product to between 68 percent and 75 percent ABV. Collect the tails and add to next batch.

5. Mature the resulting spirit in a heavily charred new American oak barrel. "Heavily charred" means until the staves of the cask start to buckle on the inside layer of the barrel (about 20 seconds of yellow flame). There will be alternatives to full-sized barrels for home distillers, discussed later, in the barrel aging section.

Basic Variations:

1. **High Rye Bourbon:**

Rye lends spicy notes to whiskey (flavors range from caraway seeds to carrot cake). To make spicier bourbon, try adding more rye, in place of the wheat in the recipe. If you want the whiskey even spicier, try removing some of the corn and replacing it with rye.

2. **Wheated Bourbon:**

Wheat makes for very smooth--but sometimes boring--whiskey. To smoothen and lighten your bourbon, try trading the rye in the recipe for wheat. You can, of course, reduce the corn and change it for wheat, as well.

Advanced:

Duplicating commercial bourbons in your kitchen can be quite tricky. Despite the 350-plus brands of bourbon made in the United States, essentially, they all come from the same 13 distilleries. These distilleries use the same type of still (a continuous column) and similar fermentation environments. As a home distiller, you are more likely to make bourbons resembling 100 year-old brands than you are to duplicate the modern products. You simply don't have access to the massive type of equipment they are using, which tends to produce a specific and uniform result.

The top commercial brands are dominated by a lot of cherry notes or rye spice, depending on the style. The estery/cherry flavor in bourbon is produced from an ester called ethyl-heptanoate. If you are attempting to mimic the commercial distilleries, you will need a yeast strain that produces high levels of this specific ester. Try Lalvin ICV-D21 to begin, and branch out from there.

To recreate the commercial bourbons, you will need to modify your still, as well. Commercial bourbon distilleries use continuous column stills with high rectification. To mimic this effect, try packing your still head with copper wool to increase rectification, or fit your still with 2 doublers.

Better yet, don't try to duplicate the commercial bourbons. At one time, there were over 10,000 distilleries across the United States, making a huge variety of different bourbons. They were using stills just like yours, along with local yeast and bacteria strains. By simply experimenting with the recipes, and not trying to duplicate the big distilleries, you can help bring back bourbon's legacy!

Oak:

According to federal regulations, bourbon must be aged in new charred American oak. You will be surprised at what a difference varying the char will do. Lighter chars mean more caramel, while deeper chars mean more almonds and dark nutty flavors. Be careful. Too much char, and you can ruin the cask. Twenty-five seconds is about maximum for a yellow flame (more on this under maturation).

Since you are not a commercial distillery, feel free to break some rules. The laws relating to new American oak are only there to protect the business interests of the big Kentucky distilleries.

Try using charred French oak for high-rye bourbon. French oak adds a lot of cinnamon character to a whiskey, and makes a fantastic, spicy high-rye bourbon.

Alternately, try a used red wine cask for wheated bourbon. It will increase the red fruity notes.

Just remember that if you were a commercial distillery, bourbons must be 51 percent corn, and aged in new charred American oak. Therefore, you cannot, technically, call these brilliant little abominations "bourbon," or the folks in Kentucky will find you!

American Rye Whiskey:

Native to the United States, American rye whiskey is a rich, dense, brick of a whiskey. Don't confuse it with Canadian rye, which is completely different. At its best, American rye whiskey is like drinking an almond-flavored carrot cake, cream cheese frosting and all! There are two main styles: single grain rye malt, and classic American rye. *Ri1* and *Rittenhouse 23* are great products to taste in order to establish a baseline of the two styles.

By law, American rye is 51 percent rye (either berries or rye malt), and it must be aged in a new, charred American oak casks. Like bourbons, the recipes include some malted barley (for enzymes that convert starch to sugar), except the 100-percent malted rye formulas.

It is highly recommended that you use a Lactobacillus bacteria culture in rye mashes, and distill as soon as the yeast in the fermentation begins to weaken. (You can tell that this is happening because fewer bubbles are produced as the yeast starts to die.) Rye grain often contains spoilage bacteria spores that emerge in the third day of fermentation. They will ruin your whiskey. The Lactobacillus and yeast can hold them at bay, but not indefinitely.

Basic Rye Recipe:

Ingredients:

1 gallon water

2 lbs. cracked rye berries

½ lb. cracked malted barley

½ lb. cracked malted rye

½ teaspoon powdered amylase enzyme

1 packet of ale yeast

2 teaspoons of yogurt or cheese making culture

Instructions:

1. Bring 1 gallon of water to 160 degrees. Stir in cracked rye berries and malted rye, followed by malted barley. Hold the temperature at 152 - 155 degrees for 1 hour. Then, add amylase and hold at temperature for an additional hour.

2. Cool the mash to 92 degrees. Transfer the resulting liquid and solids to your fermentation bucket. Add yeast AND bacteria culture. Ferment at room temperature for 2 to 3 days.

3. Distill with all the grain and yeast from the bottom of the bucket that has been poured into the still. Distill your low wines to a total ABV (alcohol by volume) of around 30 percent.

4. Discard 1 tablespoon of heads per gallon of mash. Distill your finished product to between 60 percent and 72 percent ABV (by taste). Collect tails and add to next batch.

5. Mature the resulting spirit in heavily charred new American oak. Heavily charring means until the staves of the cask start to buckle on the inside layer of the barrel (about 20 seconds of yellow flame). See the chapter on barrel aging for small-scale alternatives for home distillers.

Single Grain Rye Malt Whiskey:

Single grain rye malt is the gold standard for American whiskey. This rare and virtually extinct whiskey is a GREAT place to start. The yields on it are very low, so most distilleries don't make it commercially any longer. However, it was common 100 years ago. It is very easy to make and to get EXCELLENT results.

To make this whiskey, follow all the instructions for the basic rye whiskey. However, you will change all of the ingredients for 100 percent cracked rye malt.

You will also need to add powdered amalayse enzyme to the mix, and a Lactobacillus bacteria strain to help keep the bad bacteria at bay.

This whiskey is a spice bomb!

Advanced:

Rye whiskeys are dense whiskeys. These are the American equals to Islay scotches. For some people, these can be a little overwhelming. If your whiskey is a bit too strong for your taste, try adding some wheat to the mix. It will smoothen out the whiskey and dilute some of rye spice.

The rye grain, itself, will give you the classic rye spice notes. To get the mythical cream cheese frosting on your carrot cake of a whiskey, try adding a lot of freeze dried Lactobacillus bacteria. The bacteria will produce significant quantities of virtually tasteless lactic acid. When it ages, the lactic acid will form the ester ethyl lactate, which tastes like dairy cream.

Oak:

By law, rye whiskey must be matured in 100 percent new, American oak casks. By default, your wood options are, technically, quite limited. You will be surprised at what a difference varying the char will make. Lighter chars mean more caramel, while deeper chars mean more almonds and dark nutty flavors. However, be careful. Too much char can ruin the cask. Twenty-five seconds of yellow flame is about the maximum (more on this under maturation).

Since you are not a commercial distillery, feel free to break some rules. The laws relating to new American oak are only there to protect the business interests of the big Kentucky distilleries.

Try using charred French Oak to add a lot of cinnamon character to a whiskey. In contrast, try using a sherry cask to age your whiskey, or add a little sherry to your rye. Many commercial distilleries add sherry to sweeten and balance the spice notes of the rye.

Please see the chapter on aging for some small-scale alternatives to using 59-gallon casks for home distillers.

Pure Pot Still Irish Whisky

Native to the debatable birthplace of whiskey, pure pot still is a light, but complicated, style of whiskey. Made from a combination of malted and un-malted barley, and distilled three times, this whisky is time-consuming to make. However, the rewards can be significant. These whiskeys are crisp, clean, and can be quite complex.

There are three styles of Irish whiskey, but pure pot still is the most distinctive to Ireland. I will omit the other two, since they do not differ much from Scotch malts, which I will cover next.

Also, Irish whiskeys are distilled as a wort, not a mash. You will need either a wort strainer or some cheesecloth to separate the grain bed from the wort. This is covered in detail in the mashing chapter. If you are a home brewer, you already know how to do this step.

Basic Irish Whiskey Recipe

Ingredients:

1 gallon water

1½ lbs. cracked barley berries

1½ lbs. cracked, malted barley

1 packet of ale or lager yeast (lager yeast will make a lighter whiskey than ale yeast)

1 teaspoon of yogurt or cheese making culture

Instructions:

1. Bring ½ gallon of water to 160 degrees. Stir in cracked barley berries followed by malted barley. Hold the temperature at 152 - 155 degrees for 1

hour and 30 minutes. Strain and separate the grain from the wort. Proceed to wash twice, with ¼ gallon of water each time. The first wash will be at 165 degrees, and the second wash at 180 degrees. Combine the 2 washes with the initial wort in one pot – discard the grains after straining.

2. Cool the wash to 92 degrees. Transfer the resulting liquid to your fermentation bucket. Add yeast AND bacteria culture. Ferment at room temperature for 2 to 3 days.

3. Distill with the yeast from the bottom of the bucket. Distill your low wines to a total ABV (alcohol by volume) of around 30 percent.

4. Redistill the low wines and discard 1 tablespoon of heads per gallon of mash. Distill your second run to between 55 percent and 70 percent ABV (by taste). Collect tails and add to next fermentation.

5. Distill the resulting whiskey again, discarding a second tablespoon of heads. Distill the third run to between 80 percent and 90 percent ABV. again collecting tails to add to the next fermentation.

6. Mature the resulting spirit in charred or toasted used oak. Typically, lightly toasted, ex-white wine casks or ex-bourbon casks are used.

Advanced:

Because Irish whiskey is distilled from wort, and not mash, the ester profile of the whiskey is less affected by yeast strains, and more affected by bacteria influence. Try experimenting with various Lactobacillus strains instead of yeast types.

Oak:

Your wood options are technically unlimited with Irish whiskey. Usually ex-bourbon casks are the typical wood used to mature Irish whisky. However, you can experiment with all sorts of different types of casks. Try various white wine casks as a starting point.

Single Malt Whiskey

Native to Scotland, but now produced around the world, single malt whiskey offers the distiller an endless world of possibilities. The only rule is that you must use 100 percent malted barley. After that, "the world is your oyster." New oak, used oak, sherried oak, and wood from Sauternes wine are commonly used. Additionally, distillers use peated grain to make Islay-style whiskeys, and specialty malts to flavor lighter styles. Essentially, you can spend a lifetime experimenting, and just scratch the surface in this category.

There are two main sub-styles: peated and un-peated (Un-peated scotches are still slightly peated). It is important that you have a little peated grain in the mixture to trigger a critical chemical reaction. I will cover both recipes here, along with a lot of information in the advanced section.

NOTE: You can buy peated malt at many homebrew shops.

Basic Un-Peated Malt Recipe:

Ingredients:

1 gallon water

3 lbs. cracked malted barley

1/10 lb. cracked, peated malted barley, 40 ppm
(or 1/5 lb cracked peated malted barley, 20 ppm)

1 packet of ale yeast

1 teaspoon of yogurt or cheese making culture

NOTE: Ppm is a measure of the parts per million of phenol in the grain. Commonly, it is used as a measure of how intensely smoked the grain is. Your homebrew shop should know how to order this for you. If not, find a new homebrew shop!

Instructions:

1. Bring ½ gallon of water to 160 degrees. Stir in malted barley. Hold the temperature at 152 - 155 degrees for 1 hour 30 minutes. Strain and separate the grain from the wort. Proceed to wash twice with one-quarter gallon of water each time. The first wash will be at 165 degrees, and the second wash will be at 180 degrees. Combine the 3 washes in one pot, and discard the grains.

2. Cool the wort to 92 degrees. Transfer the resulting liquid to the fermentation bucket. Add yeast AND bacteria culture. Ferment at room temperature for 2 to 6 days.

3. Distill the wort <u>with</u> the yeast from the bottom of the bucket. Distill your low wines to a total ABV (alcohol by volume) of around 30 percent.

4. Discard 1 tablespoon of heads per gallon of mash. Then, collect the foreshots (first spirit off

the still that tastes like vodka) and save them to add to your next run.

5. Distill your finished product to between 55 percent and 72 percent ABV (by taste). Collect tails and add them to the next batch.

6. Mature in used bourbon, used sherry, or used wine casks. For small-scale alternatives to full-sized barrels please refer to the aging chapter in the back of the book.

Basic Peated Malt Recipe:

Ingredients:

1 gallon water

3 lbs. cracked, peated malted barley, 20 - 40 ppm

1 packet of ale yeast

1 teaspoon of yogurt or cheese making culture

Prepare in the same fashion as the unpeated recipe.

Advanced:

Single malts are very sensitive to small changes in the recipe. For example, the small amount of peat in the unpeated recipe is critical to form the honey notes that are so typical to scotches.

Your choices of bacteria will totally change the final product if you are doing a long fermentation (more than 3 days). Short fermentations will be different, as well. Yeast strains will have major impacts on shorter fermentations. Try Belgian ale yeast to start. Then, begin experimenting with other high-ester yeast strains.

Single malts can be anything that your imagination can dream up, which is what makes them so interesting. Feel free to bend a few traditions.

Oak:

Your wood options are limitless. Though usually matured in ex-bourbon wood or ex-sherry casks, there are no rules. If you can dream it up, it's fair game. Many distillers experiment with barrels that held exotic wines like Madeiras, Ports, Sauternes, and Cabernets. Alternatively, you could try ex-cognac casks or ex-rum wood.

Each single malt is so unique that you will want to be very careful in selecting your cask type. I recommend sampling your whiskey in a small glass with a few drops of the wine or spirit held in a previous cask to see if they pair well. Personally, I tried this with *Leviathan*, and found that port wine paired horribly! Conversely, late harvest Cabernet and Semillion worked perfectly.

Beyond the prior contents, keep in mind that French oak will add a cinnamon note to your whiskey, and American oak will add a vanilla background.

For small-scale alternatives for home distillers, please turn to the aging chapter in the back of the book.

Hopped Whiskey:

Native to the United States, and invented in the 2000s, hopped whiskey is a brilliant abomination! Directly related to the homebrew movement, this is where you take your favorite home brewed beer and distill it into whiskey.

I am not going to give you a recipe, simply because there are so many possible beer recipes that can be applied. I put this section in for advanced home brewers who have a favorite beer that they already make, and want to try turning it into whiskey.

It's worth noting that both *Charbay* and *Corsair* distilleries have taken this idea and turned it into a commercial enterprise.

Since this is not a recognized style that has rules, you can basically do whatever you want. Try distilling a double IPA, a triple Belgian, or your favorite *Hefferveisen*.

STEP 2.
GETTING STARTED

GRAIN MASHING AND WORT STRAINING

Now that you have read the first section of the book, chosen your still, selected a recipe, and bought your supplies, you are ready to begin making whiskey. This chapter is all about starch conversion: the first step to making grain fermentable. Before you get started, a quick checklist is needed to make sure that you are ready.

Checklist:

1. Grain
2. Yeast packets
3. Bacteria culture (optional)
4. Large cooking pot
5. Plastic bucket and lid for fermenting
6. Mash tun or cheesecloth for making wort (optional)
7. Thermometer
8. Still
9. Hotplate or alternate heating system
10. Alcohol hydrometer
11. Graduated cylinder
12. Funnel
13. Empty bottles and caps
14. Sugar hydrometer (saccharometer)

MASHING GRAIN

Yeast eat simple sugars and make alcohol. If you were an atheist before reading this book, this simple fact might make you believe in God! Unfortunately, even yeast has its limitations. Yeast cannot eat starch, and they definitely cannot eat un-cracked grains. Therefore, we have to help them do their work by first cracking the grains, and then converting the starch into maltose and glucose--simple sugars yeast can readily eat. This chapter will walk you through this process, step-by-step.

CRACKING GRAIN

Once you have bought your grains, you will need to mill them (or crack them) into a "grist" that can be cooked into a "mash." You can buy your own grain cracker at the homebrew shop, or you can simply ask the shop owner to crack them for you. All homebrew shops offer a grain cracking service for people who do not own their own mill.

For spirits production, you will want a "fine grist," which is somewhere between normal brewing grist and flour. Pure flour is bad, since it will "gum up" your equipment, and beer-brewing grist is a little too coarse to get the maximum sugar conversion from the grain. However, don't worry too much about the texture of the cracked grain, as it is minor point. All that you really need is for the grain husk to be broken so that the yeast can get to the starch.

NOTE: Bourbon makers, you can save a lot of money by purchasing cornmeal (polenta is preferable) from your local grocery store. There is no difference between commercial cornmeal and that which is sold in homebrew shops, EXCEPT that you need to check the ingredients to make sure you're not buying corn that has been treated with chemicals. The ingredient list should say 100 percent ground corn. Preservatives and lye treatments will make the corn inedible for the yeast.

MAKING MASH

If your recipe calls for a "mash," then this is your next step. Should your recipe say to make a "wort," you will skip these instructions and proceed to the next sub-section.

NOTE: Before you begin, check to make sure you have an accurate thermometer. Temperatures in this phase **must** *be controlled precisely.*

NOTE: Even if you recipe calls for a wort, you may want to try it as a mash. You will get different results with each, and it can be an interesting experiment.

Now that you have your bags of milled grains, the next step is to convert the starch to maltose (yeast food). To do this, we need to activate the amylase enzymes in the malted barley by heating the grains in water to 152 degrees.

Begin by measuring out the grains for your recipe. Meanwhile, bring 1 gallon of water (or more if you are making a bigger batch) to 160 degrees in your 2 to 3- gallon cooking pot.

Once the water is heated to 160 degrees, turn off the burner and stir in your milled grain. You will notice that adding the grain lowers the temperature of the mash to about 152 degrees, which is exactly where we want it. If the temperature is less than 152 degrees, gently heat it to 152, while stirring continuously. Let the grain soak for an hour in the warm water to hydrate the starches. If you recipe calls for adding amylase enzyme go ahead and add it after the hydration period. Next, begin sugar conversion by carefully controlling the temperature to stay between 150 degrees and 155 degrees for the next 30 – 45 minutes.

NOTE: Even if your recipe does not call for added amylase, it is often a good idea to add it as an "insurance policy". The substance is harmless, and, anyway, it is extracted from barley.

Maintain the temperature for 30 to 45 minutes. It's not a problem if the temperature goes up to 155 degrees, or down to 145. Just remember to stir the pot any time that you have turned on the burner. Scorched mash is not usable.

After 30 to 45 minutes, the mash will begin to taste like sweet tea. That sweetness is the maltose sugar that you have just made from the starch.

NOTE: You cannot tell when the sugar conversion is complete by tasting it. Once the sugar reaches a certain concentration, it will taste the same, even if you double the sugar concentration. Only your sugar hydrometer can tell you what concentration is present.

After 45 minutes, the mashing is complete. You will now need to cool it rapidly. If you let it cool on its own, it will take all night and there is a good chance you will end up with a bacteria or wild yeast contamination.

To cool the wort, set the cooking pot in a sink full of cold water, and simply let it sit for an hour or two, checking the temperature and stirring every 30 minutes. Once the temperature is below 92 degrees, proceed to the next chapter, "Fermenting."

NOTE: If you are a home brewer, you may have a whirlpool chiller, which will also work. A plate chiller will not, since the mash is too thick to fit between the plates.

MAKING WORT

If your recipe calls for a "wort," then this is your next step. If your recipe calls for a "mash," this step is unnecessary.

*NOTE: Before you begin, check to make sure you have an accurate thermometer. Temperatures in this phase must be controlled **precisely**.*

NOTE: Even if you recipe calls for a wort, you may want to try it as a mash. You will get different results with each, and it can be fun to experiment.

Now that you have your bags of milled grains, the next step is to convert the starch to maltose (yeast food). To do this, we need to activate the amylase enzymes in the malted barley by heating the grains in water to 152 degrees.

Begin by measuring the grains for your recipe. Meanwhile, bring one-half of the water called for in your recipe to 157 degrees in your 2 to 3-gallon cooking pot.

Once the water is heated to 157 degrees, stir in the milled grain. You should have just enough water in the pot to cover the grain. You will notice that adding the grain lowers the temperature of the mash to about 152 degrees, which is exactly where you want it. If the temperature is less than 152 degrees, gently heat it to 152, while stirring continuously. Let the grain sit in the warm water for 1 hour to hydrate the starches. After the one-hour hydration period, bring the temperature to a precise 152 degrees. If your recipe calls for added amylase enzyme, now is the time to add it.

NOTE: Even if your recipe does not call for added amylase, it is often a good idea to add it, anyway, as an "insurance policy." This substance is harmless, and it is extracted from barley.

Maintain the temperature for 30 to 45 minutes. It's not a problem if the temperature goes up to 155 degrees, or down to 145 degrees. Just remember to stir the pot any time you have turned on the heat. Burned mash is not usable.

After 30 to 45 minutes, the mash will begin to taste like sweet tea. That sweetness is the maltose sugar you have just made from the starch.

NOTE: You cannot tell when the sugar conversion is complete by taste. Once the sugar reaches a certain concentration, it will taste the same, even if you double the sugar concentration. Only your sugar hydrometer can tell you what concentration is present.

After 45 minutes, the mashing is complete. You will now need to separate the wort from the grain by straining and washing, also know as "lautering." There are several ways to do this. If you're an experienced home brewer, you probably have an elaborate "mash tun." However, for people who don't own one of these gadgets, the easiest thing to do is place a thick bed of cheesecloth on the bottom of a vegetable steamer or caldron, and simply strain the liquid through the cheesecloth.

Once you have separated the sugary liquid from the grain, you will need to "wash" the grain. To do this, bring one-fourth of the water called for in the recipe to 160 degrees. Then, slowly pour the hot water over the grain and cheesecloth, and add the resulting "wash" to the sugary liquid that you strained the first time.

After completing the first washing of the grain, repeat the process with the last one-fourth of the water heated to 180-degrees. After this step, keep the liquid and dispose of the leftover grains (great fertilizer for the garden).

Once you have combined the washes, you should have approximately the amount of liquid called for in the recipe. You will now need to cool it rapidly. If you let it cool on its own, it will take all night, and there is a good chance you will end up with a bacteria or wild yeast contamination.

To cool the wash, set the cooking pot full of wort in a sink full of cold water, and simply let it sit for an hour or two, checking the temperature and stirring every 30 minutes. Once the temperature is below 92 degrees, proceed to the next chapter, "Fermenting."

NOTE: *If you are a home-brewer you may have a whirlpool chiller or a plate chiller, either of which will work well.*

NOTE: *There are many ways top do this. For alternate methods, Google "lautering."*

STEP 3.
FERMENTATION

Now that you have cooled your mash or wort to between 70 and 92 degrees, it is time to begin working nature's magic to turn that useless sugar-water into something glorious!

NOTE: Higher temperature fermentations produce more esters, which, unlike in beer making, is a good thing. Ninety degrees is an ideal temperature to start your fermentation.

First, we must establish a baseline sugar level. To do this, collect a 200 to 300-ml sample of liquid from the top of your mash or wort, and place it into your graduated cylinder. Then, float the sugar hydrometer (saccharometer) in the cylinder. The hydrometer will float to a line on the meter indicating the sugar level. Depending on the brand, it will read in potential alcohol, specific gravity, or brix. All three of these measurements are different units of measurement that explain the same thing. From this point on, I am going to refer to them in potential alcohol. On the next page, I have included a conversion chart, in the event that your sugar hydrometer does not include potential alcohol.

Specific Gravity	Brix	Potential Alcohol
1.000	1.6	0.0%
1.005	2.7	0.6%
1.010	3.8	1.3%
1.015	4.9	1.9%
1.020	6.0	2.6%
1.025	7.1	3.3%
1.030	8.2	3.9%
1.035	9.3	4.6%
1.040	10.4	5.2%
1.045	11.5	5.9%
1.050	12.6	6.6%
1.055	13.7	7.2%
1.060	14.8	7.9%
1.065	15.9	8.5%
1.070	17.0	9.2%
1.075	18.1	9.9%
1.080	19.2	10.5%
1.085	20.3	11.2%
1.090	21.4	11.8%

The alcohol hydrometer is measuring sugar, not alcohol. Since the yeast cells are consuming sugar to make alcohol, the potential alcohol reading on the hydrometer will fall as the fermentation progresses. In short, if your starting potential alcohol was 10 percent, and you fermented for 2 days, and now had a potential alcohol of 3 percent, you would have made 7 percent alcohol. You are measuring the change in sugar content to estimate the alcohol content.

Your wort or mash should read from 6 percent to 10 percent potential alcohol. If you are over 10 percent, add water to dilute the sugar to within the ideal range. If you are under 6 percent, something has gone wrong (see troubleshooting in the back of the book).

The potential alcohol percentage should be under 10 percent. Alcohol levels above 10 percent will quickly kill the yeast and stop the fermentation before you finish converting the sugar into whiskey.

NOTE: Some recipes from the Internet call for much higher potential alcohol percentages and the use of special yeast strains that can ferment to higher percentages of alcohol. In my opinion, those recipes are misguided. The yeast strains employed in higher sugar whiskey fermentations (Turbo Yeast and Champagne Yeast) produce sub-par whiskeys and should be avoided.

PITCHING YEAST

With the wort or mash cooled to around 90 degrees, you are ready to start fermentation.

To do this, you must first aerate the mash or wort to ensure there is plenty of oxygen present for our "little yeasty friends." Many people use all sorts of fancy apparatuses to do this. All you really need to do is dump the mash back and forth a few times between the fermentation bucket and the pot. The splashing will add enough oxygen to the mash to get the fermentation started.

*NOTE: To the home brewers: Excess oxygen will interfere with ester formation, which is a major goal in whiskey making. It is best **not** to use bottled oxygen.*

With the mash or wort aerated, simply follow the instructions on the yeast packet for hydrating and pitching the yeast.   If you are adding your own bacteria, now is the time to add it (bacteria is discussed in depth in the next chapter).

Advanced:

Adding smaller quantities of yeast than the package calls for will slow the fermentation down and produce more esters in the finished product. Though this is beneficial, it is a gamble. The risk of spoilage bacteria or wild yeast infection goes up dramatically. If you don't mind losing a batch every now and again, this will improve your whiskey.

As soon as you add yeast, they will begin to multiply fast. In ideal conditions (like a whiskey mash), yeast will double in numbers every 2 hours. As they ferment, they will acidify the mash, thus lowering the PH of the mash from a starting PH of 5 - 6 to a final PH of 3.5. This is how they control bacteria growth, since the yeast can multiply well in low PH environments, while bacteria are somewhat inhibited in a low PH environment.

As the yeast eat, they will consume sugar and produce carbon dioxide bubbles and alcohol, along with aromatic esters and volatile acids. You can tell the fermentation is going well because a few hours after pitching yeast, you will begin to see a lot of bubbles forming in the mash. After 12 hours, the bubbles will be so intense that they will push the grain in the mash to the top to form a thick cap, or they will make a wort fizzle like soda pop.

In commercial distilleries, the cap is carefully managed for a variety of reasons. However, in a home distillery environment, you don't need to worry about it. The yeast will produce a lot of heat during this phase. In small batches, the heat will dissipate through the bucket and should not be a problem. In commercial distilleries, we need elaborate cooling systems to keep the yeast from cooking themselves to death. If you are worried about the heat, periodically take a temperature reading. Anything under 95 degrees is safe. Eighty-five degrees is ideal.

After several days of fermentation, the cap will begin to sink back into the mash. You can then take a new hydrometer reading. Your fermentation is done when the potential alcohol is below 2 percent.

You can let it ferment longer. However, you will be in a bacterial fermentation at that point. If you let it go too long, it can get overly acidic. I recommend a total fermentation time of 2 to 4 days for most whiskeys. However, there is always room for experimentation. Trial and error is how you master your art form!

SOUR MASHING

Sour mashing was originally developed as a way to slow bacteria growing in the mash by lowering the starting PH before the yeast were added. The common way of doing this is to keep some mash from the previous batch, and add it to the new one. This lowers the PH in the starting mash, and inhibits bacteria growth. It also lets the yeast focus on making alcohol, since they won't need to make as much acid to get the PH to the 3.5 mark where they are "happy."

Advanced:

As an alternative, there is another way to sour mash. To a small extent, I employ this at Lost Spirits Distillery. Initially, this is where you pitch friendly Lactobacillus bacteria, and then wait to add the yeast. The Lactobacillus bacteria will lower the PH quickly, preventing your yeast from making some of the acids they would normally make. Since the bacteria will make a different set of acids than the yeast, this can have a big effect. This will dramatically change the acid and ester profile of the whiskey. It can be very interesting, but it can also be very odd. Experimentation is king! Personally, I only do this for a short time. However, you can do it for up to a day with ever-increasing, dramatic effects.

STEP 4.

BACTERIAL FERMENTATION

This chapter is optional. Therefore, I am going to get quite technical. If you are new to making whiskey, you may wish to completely skip this chapter, along with the bacteria component of whiskey making. If you are somewhat advanced, hopefully, this will be quite enlightening.

BACKGROUND:

Complex flavors in whiskey come primarily from chemicals called esters. Esters are compounds made by chemically bonding together an alcohol molecule and an acid molecule. Esters are formed in every step of the whiskey-making process. Yeast strains make them, and free acids in solution will eventually form into esters in the aging process.

Free acids, which are the building blocks for esters, can come from many places in the whiskey-making process. They come from the oak, the yeast, and the bacteria. However, the bacterial effect is the least-discussed fact in the industry.

Lactobacillus bacteria produce a wide range of volatile acids when they consume sugar in the fermentation. Though all Lactobacillus produce large amounts of lactic acid, each strain will produce a different range of other acids. Lactic acid esterifies with ethanol into ethyl lactate, which tastes like butter cream. However, the other acids they make can esterify into flavors ranging from jasmine and violets, to strawberries and honey.

Under certain circumstances, Lactobacillus will even consume other acids already in the fermentation and change them into different ones.

This can lead to interesting synergistic effects between strains. The range of flavors you can create in your whiskey by managing these" little guys" is nearly endless. When combined with a mastery of the other components of the process, you can, literally, build and stack flavorful effects to make whiskeys so dense that they will mystify even the most experienced palettes in the business.

PRACTICAL APPLICATION:

Lactobacillus is highly active in the beginning, and at the end, of the fermentation. However, it is somewhat dormant while the yeast is highly active.

In the first hours of fermentation, the Lactobacillus is rapidly multiplying. Even if you don't add your own bacteria, the spores of Lactobacillus Thermophilus are on the grain. They will survive the heat of the sugar-conversion phase. Additional strains will also float into the mash in the air. In our area, this usually means Lactobacillus Sanfrancisco, but your region will have its own native strains.

Once the yeast takes over, the Lactobacillus dramatically slows its reproduction rate, due to the low PH of the solution created by the yeast. They don't die. They just multiply considerably slower, doubling in numbers only once every 12 to 18 hours.

In the final phase of the fermentation, the yeast begin to die, at which point the Lactobacillus thrive, consuming nutrients left by the dead yeast and scavenging any residual sugar. As the Lactobacillus eat, they throw off significant amounts of acids that will later form flavorful esters in the whiskey.

As a home whiskey maker, you can easily manage their numbers by adding freeze-dried bacteria strains to the fermentation. Lactobacillus strains are available commercially from many sources. You can buy them in yogurt making kits, cheese making kits, probiotic tablets from health food stores, and in refrigerated liquid form at homebrew shops.

If you add large amounts of them with your yeast, you are sure to increase their numbers during fermentation. You can also increase their effects by letting them multiply for several hours prior to adding the yeast to the fermentation. The bacterial effects will also be greater if you let the fermentation go longer, after the yeast has started to die. Interestingly, the bacteria's influence will change, depending on the phase of fermentation in which they are active. When they eat glucose in the mash, they produce one set of acids. They produce different flavors when they are eating dying yeast.

Experimentation is key. Each strain will produce different results. In turn, they will produce new and unique effects when added in combination with other strains. They also compete with spoilage bacteria for nutrients, so they can help protect your fermentation from bad bacteria.

I recommend that you start by adding a little freeze- dried cheese making bacteria to your mash, along with your yeast. Try www.cheesemaking.com for a large selection of different safe bacteria.

NOTE: There is such a thing as too much of a good thing. If the bacteria are left dominant for more than a day, they begin to add salty, fermented noodle notes to the whiskey. Although this can be interesting (if it goes just right and you get smoked oyster notes) usually, it does not work out well in the end result.

NOTE: A few words of caution: Lactobacillus is usually harmless. However, if you have an immune deficiency disorder, this can be dangerous. In addition, it is important to know what Lactobacillus growth smells like so you don't confuse it with spoilage bacteria. Lactobacillus produces mostly lactic acid, which has virtually no smell. When Lactobacillus is very active, the wash will start to smell acidic and almost indefinably citric (grapefruit, and lemon aromas). Spoilage bacteria will smell like vomit or rancid cheese. Do not confuse the two! If your mash smells like rancid cheese or vomit, throw it away. Not only are these bad aromas, some of the bacteria that produce them can be dangerous.

STEP 5.
FIRST DISTILLATION

THE STRIPPING RUN

Your fermentation is complete, and now its time to distill. The adrenaline is pumping, and the fun begins!

The first step is to fill your still with the mash or wort. It's important to make sure you collect all the "lees" from the bottom of the bucket and add them to the still. Lees are the caked-on material from the bottom of the fermentation bucket. For the most part, it is half-dead yeast, and it has the consistency of peanut butter. The lees play an import role in the flavor of the whiskey.

NOTE: Not everyone agrees with me. Some distilleries intentionally remove the lees.

Once the pot is filled two-thirds of the way, set the still on a hot plate. Never fill a still more than two-thirds of the way. If you do, the mash can foam and plug the condenser, creating a safety hazard.

Next, set the still head firmly in place (it should just slip in) and seal the seam along with any leaks by using flour paste. You can make your own flour paste by mixing water and flour until it forms a thick paste. Once the still heats, the paste will harden and form a tight seal. If anything goes horribly wrong, the flour will give way and the head will pop off of the still.

Then, fill the condenser (the pot with a coil in it) with cold water and turn on the heat.

It will take several hours for your still to begin to distill. The mash will have to heat up to over 170 degrees before you see any action. Be sure to heat it very slowly, since you don't want to burn the mash. It's easy to do, and it will ruin the whiskey.

Initially, the distillate will exit the still with a very high concentration of alcohol (over 75%). Over time, the percentage of alcohol will fall, as more and more water begins to pass over the still. You will want to keep collecting for quite a long time. This distillation is an intermediate step, not a finished product. Don't worry about collecting too much.

Since this is a stripping run, you don't need to do much except watch it run. No heads cut is necessary during this initial run. During this time, the condenser will absorb the heat from the distillate, and the water on the top of the condenser will get very hot. This is all right. However, the bottom of the condenser should always be cool to the touch. If the bottom begins to heat up, you will need to add new cold water. Most condensers have holes at the bottom and top to allow you to exchange hot water from the top for new cold water added to the bottom. If necessary, you can always add ice to the condenser.

Keeping your condenser cool is an important safety measure. If the bottom of the condenser overheats, alcohol vapor will begin to come out of condenser. This vapor is very explosive, and it can start a bad fire, or worse. Always watch the still!

Collect the distillate for the next several hours, and consistently check the alcohol percentage of the total that you have collected by using your alcohol hydrometer. To do this, pour some of the distillate into your graduated cylinder. Drop the hydrometer in and it will float, showing the proof (or percentage) on a line at the point where the

hydrometer emerges from the distillate.

You should continue to mix all of the distillate together, and take readings until the total proof reads 45 to 60 (22.5%-30% ABV). Once you reach 44 to 50 proof, the distillate will be a hazy, murky, semi-clear liquid. This is called low wines. Do not let your nose pass judgment. Low wines often don't tell you very much about the whiskey. They always smell acidic and "off."

The most important things to remember are: always keep the condenser cool, never walk away from a running still, and keep the heat low to avoid burning the mash. Expect to spend most of the day with your still. Over time, you will form a bond with your still that only the authorities can break!

STEP 6.
SECOND
DISTILLATION

THE FINISHING RUN

The moment of truth is upon you. All of your hard work is about to become something you can actually drink!

Finishing runs require constant attention. Be sure that you have 2 to 3 hours without distractions so that you can focus on the very important work at hand. Turn off the television, lock the screaming kids in the basement, and give the dog some of the last whiskey you made. All your attention needs to be on the still during this phase.

Once you have cleaned your still from the stripping run, fill it back up with the low wines, and reassemble it (flour paste, and all).

The proof of the spirit will initially be very high (80 percent to 90 percent alcohol) so be conscious of any nearby fire hazards. Turn on your still, and get ready for action! Since the still does not contain any solids this time, you may run the heat on high.

DURING THIS FINAL DISTILLATION, YOU MUST COLLECT THE FIRST TABLESPOON OF DISTILATE PER GALLON OF MASH OR WORT AND THROW IT AWAY. This is called the "heads cut." The first tablespoon per gallon of mash of the finishing run is poisonous and cannot be left in your finished product. Be sure to pay close attention to your still, since finishing runs go much faster than stripping runs. If you are distracted, you might miss the critical moment, and have to throw away the entire batch.

NOTE: if this happens, you can try adding everything back into the still and starting over, but it's never the same.

Once you have collected and discarded this first portion of the distillate, you can begin collecting finished product. If your recipe calls for "foreshots" to be collected, you will want to taste the initial distillate until it becomes less like vodka and takes on a richer flavor. You can either discard the foreshots, or add them to the next batch.

As you collect the finished product, dip the back end of a spoon (or your pinky) into the stream and frequently try small drops of your spirit. You will taste the distillate changing by the minute. Each one of the flavor compounds will separate and come out at different times as the proof of the distillate changes.

In addition to taste, use your hydrometer to check the proof of what you have collected. Distillations are done when your taste buds tell you that they are done. In general, most distillations are complete between 52 percent AND 72 percent ABV. Most styles are closer to 72 percent than 52 percent.

Distillations are close to finished when you begin to taste "tails." "Tails" are a low-proof distillate that comes off the still after most of the alcohol has been distilled. They contain a mixture of water and higher alcohols, like propanol, an amyl alcohol. You want a little bit of the "tails" in your spirit. They lend sweet flavors and round out the whole product. However, if you collect too much, you can ruin the distillate. Knowing when to draw the line is a fine art, and it takes experience to master it.

"Tails" will initially taste very sweet, and can taste quite good. However, you will find that if you collect too much of them, the spirit will become "muddy" tasting. If you collect too little, the spirit will be dry and hot. Knowing when to make your "tails cut" is, by far, the most critical part of the entire process. A perfect fermentation, with perfect ingredients, and a perfect stripping run, can easily be ruined by a poor tail's cut. Unfortunately, every recipe is different, and every still is different, so there is no hard-and-fast rule as to when to make the cut. Personally, I recommend that you frequently taste the spirit that you have collected. Try to make a judgment based upon flavor.

Take meticulous notes during the finishing run. You may find that at 65 percent you loved the spirit, but by the time it dropped to 63 percent you no longer liked it. If you have meticulous notes, you know to repeat the fermentation...but, this time, stop at 65 percent ABV.

Finishing runs happen fast, so expect to ruin some of them. As long as you take great notes, you will know what to do next time. A wise man once said, "The secret to life is making good decisions." When asked how to do that, he answered: "...by learning from lots of bad decisions." With each botched finishing run, you will be one step closer to a good one!

NOTE: Irish whiskey making will have three distillations. The first is a standard stripping run. The second is the finishing run, and a third run is an additional finishing run, where the final cut around 90 percent ABV.

*NOTE: Do not leave the heads lying around in a glass. These are extremely **poisonous** and you don't want someone drinking them by mistake. As a habit, I simply drop the heads on my least favorite weed in the garden. Heads are very volatile and evaporate quickly. This ensures that no one accidentally drinks poison.*

NOTE: If you get a pounding headache and hangover after drinking your whiskey, increase the size of the heads cut from 1 tablespoon per gallon of mash to 2 tablespoons. Trace amounts of methanol (the poison in the heads) are the cause of the headaches associated with hangovers. Each type of yeast will produce a slightly different amount of methanol, so with a little caution, you can quickly fix a hangover problem. In general, removing 1 tablespoon per gallon of heads is enough to eliminate all of the methanol.

NOTE: You can collect the tails, and add them to the next low wines that you make. In that way, you get all of the alcohol you made. However, you don't want to add tails from corn whiskey to a malt whiskey. Keep them separated if you are making more than one style of whiskey.

Step 7.

Maturation

CELLAR AGING

You have made your perfect whiskey, and now it is time to age it. This can be done a number of ways. To do this successfully on a small scale will require some creativity.

Of course, the best way to deal with aging is to formulate a perfect micro-batch. Then, buy a much larger still, and fill a full-sized 53 to 59-gallon cask, which you set in the basement. However, for most casual whiskey makers, this is out of the question. Knowing this, I have tried to outline some creative alternatives at the end of this chapter.

TYPES OF OAK

Each type of oak lends its own set of flavors and aromas, based on the constituent acids generated from the lignin and hemi-cellulose content of that species. What this means for the distiller is that each sub-species of oak is going to make a unique and different whiskey. Below is a list of the 5 available types, and their generally recognized characteristics.

These characteristics are only 1 part of the equation. How you toast or char the oak has a massive impact on the end flavors derived from it. Also, used oak will have a lot of flavors from the previous contents, on top of the flavors derived from the type of oak and the charring.

There are laws relating to which sub-species can be used for certain types of whiskey. Of course, there are laws against distilling whiskey in your home as well....

American Oak

--Strong vanilla notes, woody resin, light brown spice, and tannic.

French Oak

--Strong cinnamon, lots of brown spice, light vanilla, moderately tannic.

Limousin Oak

--Very strong vanilla, some brown spice

Hungarian Oak

--Vanilla and earthy chocolate notes, peppery

Mongolian Oak

--Caramel vanilla, floral, aromatic

TOASTING/CHARRING

Barrel toasting and charring is essential to the aging process. The flame breaks down the hemicellulose and lignin in the wood to form volatile acids which easterfy into a range of flavors in the whiskey. If the cask was not charred or toasted, the whiskey would hardly age at all in the barrel.

How you approach toasting or charring the cask has a HUGE effect on the final product. A light toast will bring out more of the individual oak species' characteristics, like vanilla for American oak, and cinnamon for French oak. A heavy char will bring out a lot of dark, smoky, and nutty characteristics that tend to make the subtle differences between the oak sub-species less important.

Personally, I gauge the level of char based upon the number of seconds the wood produced a yellow flame. To clarify this statement: When you char a cask, you are using a propane torch that has a blue flame. Once the wood ignites, it will produce a yellow flame indicating that the wood is actually burning.

Light Toast

--Torch until a yellow flame is visible, then extinguish

Strong caramel notes, praline, cashews

Medium Toast

--Torch until a yellow flame is visible for 5 seconds, then extinguish

Praline, light almonds, sweet

Heavy Toast

--Torch until a yellow flame is visible for 10 seconds, then extinguish

Rubbery, slightly bitter

Light Char

--Torch until the wood is partially blackened (usually a yellow flame is visible for 15 seconds, but it is better to use the wood-blackening as the indicator, instead of the flame)

Sweet, almonds, desserts, slightly smoky

Heavy Char

--Torch until the wood is blackened and splitting apart (usually a yellow flame is visible for 25 seconds, but it is better to use the wood-blackening as the indicator, instead of the flame)

Dark barrel-char notes, almonds, desserts, smoke, dark caramel

Over-Charred (ruined)

--Yellow flame for 30 plus seconds

Whiskey tastes like rancid butter

BARREL CHEMISTRY:

Barrel chemistry can be broken down into three distinct parts. Although these things happen at the same time, they are distinct chemical reactions.

Extraction:

Extraction is the process of the high proof spirit pulling acids out of the wood. When barrels are toasted or charred, some of the wood is broken down into acids. These acids include, but are not limited to, vanillic acid, cinnimic acid, acetic acid, and tannic acid. When the high proof alcohol (barreling is done at 55 percent to 62.5 percent ABV) comes into contact with the wood, some of these acids are dissolved into the spirit, thus adding color and texture from tannic acid, and flavors from the rest. Initially, these acids combine on the palette to taste woody, dry, and hot. However, over time, they interact with alcohol and oxygen change into fruity esters.

Oxidization:

Over time, small amounts of air seep into the barrel through the porous surface. This is called "breathing," and it happens as the seasons change. In the summer, the alcohol expands, causing the barrel to "exhale." In the winter, the liquid contracts, creating a vacuum that causes the barrel to "inhale" fresh air. This air brings oxygen into contact with the acids extracted from the oak and the acids that came from the fermentation. Gradually, those acids bond with the alcohol and oxygen to form esters, the sweet fruity and floral aromas that we spoke about earlier.

Concentration:

Perhaps, the least important part of the aging process is concentration. Over time, some of the alcohol and water in the barrel is lost through the breathing process. This is commonly called "the angels share." When this happens, it causes the flavors in the barrel to become more concentrated. However, this part of the process is often overstated. In the life of a whiskey, perhaps 5 percent of the contents are lost to "the angels share," so it is not as drastic as you might think. Knowing this information, as a hobby producer, you have a few choices. You can try to make enough to fill a barrel. You can buy mini-barrels, although these have their problems, or you can explore aging in glass with small wooden cubes (a technique often used to test results in commercial distilleries). I discourage people from working with wood chips, since they really don't react the same way as oak in a cask.

FULL-SIZE CASKS

New Casks

If you have the money, will, and desire to produce 55 gallons of spirit, by all means go right ahead! You can buy excellent new barrels from coopers in Napa, Missouri, Kentucky, and Virginia. If you are making a malt whiskey, you will probably wish to seek out used barrels. Ex-bourbon casks and ex-California wine casks are readily available on the secondary market.

For new casks, simply tell the cooper to give you a medium to heavy char. Wait for the delivery, and fill it with whiskey that has been diluted to 55 percent for American whiskeys, and 62.5 percent for malts and Irish whiskey. Tap in a silicone bung, and screw in a steel strap across the bung to prevent the bung from accidentally coming loose. Store in a cool, dry place.

Used Casks

If you are using the ex-wine casks, be careful to check that the wine flavors work well with your whiskey. You wouldn't want to ruin 55 gallons of product into which you have invested thousands of dollars. As a rule, I add 5 to 10 drops of the wine from the cask to a dram of my whiskey. If the flavors of the wine and the whiskey pair well, then it is safe to proceed to filling the full-sized cask. More often than not, the wine does **not** pair well, so take your time and hand-select your oak carefully.

Once the cask is selected, you will need to buy a barrel hoop driver. This hand tool will let you take a barrel apart and put it back together. Once you get the barrel home, you will need to screw in a brace board across the lid. This is so that the lid does not fall apart when you open the cask. Simply place a small board perpendicular to the staves on the lid, and place a series of stainless screws through the top board and into the barrel lid. This way, it can't fall apart. Remember that barrels don't have glue in them so the staves can fall apart very easily when they are disassembled.

With your board screwed into the lid, it is now time to tip the barrel on end, and remove the nails that hold the top 4 hoops in place. Next remove the hoops and open the barrel. You will do this by whacking the hoops with a hammer and hoop driver. Once they are off, half of the cask will open up, and the lid will fall into the barrel.

Remove the lid, and put the hoops back on without the lid. To accomplish this, simply place the hoops as far down as they will go and then begin hitting them with the hoop driver. Once the barrel is back together, you will need to wash it thoroughly. The lees from the wine will be caked onto the inside of the cask. You must remove them. I use a copper scrubber and a hose to do this. Be prepared to spend about a half-day washing a barrel.

Once the cask is clean, you will need to lightly char the barrel. To do this, you will need minimum of a 250,000 BTU propane torch (often called a roofing torch.) You will now run the torch on low, and gently heat the staves of the cask, section by section, until wine and sap begins to seep out of the stave and caramelize on the surface of the oak. As soon as that happens, move the torch to the next section.

Once you have finished, you will need to remove the 4 hoops again, and this time, reassemble with the lid in place. You will need a friend to hold the lid in place while you hammer down the rings. You may wish to add a tap so that you can sample the contents of the barrel from time to time. The tap is a simple stainless steel or lead-free brass valve with ½-inch threading. Drill a hole in the barrel lid the same size as the threading, and screw in the tap. Once the wood swells from the liquid, it will make the snug fit watertight.

Now, simply fill the cask with whiskey, tap in a silicone bung, and screw a steel strap over the bung to ensure it does not come loose. Store in a cool dry place.

NOTE: If the wood is not wet, it will not be watertight. If the cask sat dry for any length of time, you will want to check it for leaks, prior to filling it with precious whiskey. If it does leak, you will want to fill it with water for several days until the leak stops.

NOTE: If the hoops are not back in their original position, the barrel will leak. You need to keep hammering until the hoops are back where they started. The nails that hold the hoops in place should be replaced.

MINI-CASKS

New miniature barrels are readily available. The problem with these mini-casks is the exposed surface area is much greater in a small barrel than it is in a full-sized cask. This causes the wood to lend more extractives to the product than you would normally expect, while not accelerating the oxidization process. This is not as big of a problem if you are working with 10 to 15-gallon quarter casks, since these make a distinct style of whiskey that is very oaky, but not unpleasant.

These don't work very well when they are the ½-gallon or 1-gallon size. These "baby casks" will overpower the spirit with wood flavors within a few short weeks.

For malt whiskey makers, there is also a used mini-cask option. *Tutiltown Distillery* in NY produces bourbons in miniature casks (5 to 15-gallon). Without much difficulty, you should be able to contact them to find out how to purchase a few barrels. These casks work just like the big ones, so please read the instructions for charring, as listed above.

AGING IN GLASS

Though illegal for commercial producers of whiskey, moonshiners have long gotten around the barrel problem by aging in glass. They do this by adding small oak cubes to bottles of whiskey, periodically opening the bottles to let in fresh air, and then shaking them up to aerate the whiskey. Though this may not seem as romantic a notion as a mini-barrel, it does function. The extraction process works the same way and the ester formation can be induced through the addition of fresh air. Just remember that only a tiny amount of oak would be needed to mimic the amount of exposed surface area in a cask (about 3 1-cm cubes per bottle). Remember to leave some room in the top for air.

You could also experiment with soaking your oak cubes in various wine types to add the used wine cask effect. Sherry wood works wonders for almost all whiskey.

PART 4:

ADDITIONAL USEFUL INFORMATION

BASIC GLOSSARY OF TERMS:

Mash – Oatmeal-like mixture of grain and water made ready for fermentation

Mash Bill – The grain proportions used in a given recipe. E.g. Bryan's Bourbon: 70% corn, 10% rye, and 20% malted barley

Wort – Strained mash containing only the liquid and sugars of the mash, but not the grain

Wash – Another word for wort

Distiller's Beer – Another word for wort or mash

Lees – The layer of sticky yeast sitting on the bottom of a fermented mash or wort

Malting – The process of inducing and halting germination in grain to produce enzymes -- necessary for fermentation

Cooking or Mashing – The process of heating the mash to a specific temperature to activate the enzymes created during the malting

Pitching yeast or bacteria – The term for adding a living organism to your mash

Heads – The first tablespoon per gallon of mash of liquid to come off the still (notably poisonous and always discarded)

Hearts – This is the part we keep to drink! The middle cut of a distillation, between the heads and tails

Tails – The highly dilute alcohol, which comes out last from the still

Stripping Run – The first distillation, where the mash is turned into low wines

Low Wines – The murky-clear liquid that is the product of the stripping run, typically 22 to 30 percent alcohol

Finishing Run (or Spirit Run) – The second distillation where low wines are turned into high wines

High Wines – Newly distilled whiskey spirit, typically between 55 percent and 85 percent alcohol

Racking – The process of filtration where gravity and time are used to separate sediment from liquid, without damaging the spirit

Fermenter - The vessel used to ferment grain, usually just a bucket

Cap – The solid grain bits floating on top of the fermentation, that have been forced up by the carbon dioxide coming from the fermentation

Pot – The body of the still

Condenser – The cooling apparatus at the end of a still. Usually, just a coil in a small bucket of water

Neck – The part of the still that comes up and connects the pot to the condenser

Lyne Arm – Another word for neck

Swan's Neck – Another word for neck

TROUBLE SHOOTING

FERMENTATION NEVER TOOK

If yeast packets sit in the sun for long periods of time, the yeast can die. Try re-pitching new, fresh yeast.

NOTE: Pesticides or preservatives on the grain can also cause this problem. Be sure that your grain was not treated.

STUCK FERMENTATION

This is where the fermentation initially started, but stopped before the potential alcohol fell to 2 percent, or lower. This can happen for a variety of reasons. The most common reasons are lack of oxygen in the mash, or too high of a starting sugar concentration.

The initial troubleshooting strategy is to first try splashing the mash back and forth between 2 buckets to introduce new oxygen. Then, re-pitch with new yeast. If the fermentation is stuck due to excess sugar at the onset, you can try diluting the mash with warm water, and then re-pitching new yeast. You can also go ahead and try distilling what you have made, knowing that you may not get anything usable. Next time, pay closer attention to the sugar content. Anything over 10 percent potential alcohol is too much.

Stuck fermentations cannot always be cured. This is because yeast emits chemical signals when they are sick that tell other yeast not to reproduce. Unfortunately, if this happens you will usually need to start over. If you are working with a big batch, you can try to remove the mash from the lees, and then re-pitch without the lees. Sometimes, this can save the batch, since most of the yeast live at the bottom of the tank in the lees.

Just know that this is a "court of last resort," and success is far from guaranteed.

FERMENTATION SMELLS LIKE VOMIT

This problem is caused by spoilage bacteria, either from the air, or more likely, from spores on the grain. Start over, but this time sanitize everything, and try pitching double or triple the yeast along with adding friendly bacteria. The objective is to overwhelm the harmful bacteria with friendly organisms.

NOTE: If you catch this very early at the point when you aren't quite sure that it's vomit you smell, you can sometimes fix it. Many of the spoilage bacteria are strict anaerobes, meaning that oxygen is toxic to them. Try splashing the mash back and forth between buckets. There is a good chance that the bacteria will die, and the fermentation can be saved. Strangely enough, sometimes this makes for great whiskeys. The spoilage smell can form fruity esters, over time, in the cask. Strawberry notes in a whiskey are directly related to butyric acid, which also produces the vomit smell. Of course, if the vomit smell is strong, throw it away. Nothing will ever rescue that!

DISTILLATE TASTES LIKE BUCKWHEAT SOUP

This is caused when friendly bacteria are allowed to ferment too long. Repeat the process, but distill sooner--before the bacteria is out of hand!

DISTILLATE TASTES TOO HOT, WITH AN ALCOHOL BURN

This is caused because the acid content is too high in relation to the ester content. The whiskey will eventually age out and taste good. However, next time, try using a different yeast strain that

87

produces more esters during fermentation. Also, make sure that you have 4 percent to 5 percent amino acid content in the mash. You can do this by either adding amino acid supplements, or by fermenting with some grain left in the mash.

SMOKE COMING OUT OF THE CONDENSER AND DISCOLORED DISTILLATE

This is caused because you burned the mash. There is no remedy. Throw it away, and start over. Next time, be careful to heat more gently. Try adding extra water to the still with the mash to make things more fluid.

GRAY OR BLACK MOLD GROWING ON THE CAP IN THE FERMENTATION BUCKET

This problem is not generally fixable. If a significant amount of distiller's mold has grown on the fermentation, it will make the distillate taste "swampy." However, if you catch it soon enough, you can punch the cap back into the mash and mix it up, thus killing the mold.

If you have this problem consistently, try punching the cap down 2 times a day.

FERMENTATION SMELLS LIKE RANCID CHEESE

This is due to a wild yeast called *Brettanomyces*. "Brett" is always present in the air, and it can spontaneously ferment. Some breweries actually do this on purpose, but usually, you will want to begin again. Next time, pitch more yeast, sooner, to prevent the "Brett" from gaining a foothold in your fermentation.

If you consistently have this problem, try tripling the amount of yeast that you use, and pitch immediately after the temperature cools to 92 degrees. Also, try speeding up the cooling process, since the "Brett" is finding its way into the fermentation during cooling.

DISTILLATE TASTES LIKE PAINT THINNER

This is due to a common ester called ethyl acetate. Often, a central flavor to bourbon whiskey, it can be unpleasant, if made in excess. This is easy to manage because the ester will bond to phenolic acids in solution, forming a new, longer chain ester that tastes like honey.

To perform this feat, make sure your oak is heavily charred, and wait for the barrel to do its magic. If the paint thinner note is still over-powering, you can fix it in the future by adding a little smoked barley to your mash bill. The smoke aromas are phenolic acids, and they will trigger the chemical reaction that remedies the paint thinner note.

This reaction is the main difference between scotches and other whiskeys.

BLUE DISTILLATE

Because stills are made of copper, they can form green or blue deposits that can dissolve into the spirit. These heavy metal deposits are not an issue in the pot of the still, since the copper is not volatile. It does not travel with the alcohol vapor. However, the distillate can collect heavy metal deposits as it flows down the condenser.

NOTE: This is not a problem for low wines only finished spirit.

These copper deposits can be easily identified because they will turn the distillate green or blue. If you see your finished spirit has a blue tint, simply clean your equipment and redistill the spirit. The copper deposits will then be removed from the spirit, and it will be safe to drink.

Unlike heads cuts, copper deposits are not extraordinarily toxic. However, they can build up in the system and cause health problems. Consequently, it is best not to drink blue whiskey.

HANGOVERS

You drank your own whiskey and thought: *What did I do to myself? I woke up with a pounding headache!* This problem is caused by trace methanol in the distillate. This can be easily fixed by taking a larger heads cut. As another remedy, try distilling more slowly in the first phase of the finishing run. This will more effectively help separate the methanol from the ethanol.

If you also drank commercially made booze in the same night, don't be so quick to blame yourself. For reasons that I don't understand, some commercial distilleries are sloppy about leaving in the trace methanol.

NOTE: Some people claim that excess tails can cause hangovers. Though I have not found this to be the case, you can try collecting less tails in your finishing run, and see if that helps.

Made in the USA
Middletown, DE
15 February 2016